# STRENGTH FOR THE JOURNEY

## 30 Days of Scripture and Prayer for Fathers

### Karen Kazimer Shockley

**Karens Words**

*To the fathers who rise early and stay up late,
who lead with courage, love with humility,
and pray when no one sees. To the men who choose integrity
over applause,
faithfulness over comfort,
and legacy over momentary gain. To every dad striving not just
to be a good man,
but a godly one. This book is for you. May these pages strengthen
your hands,
steady your heart,
and remind you that your quiet faithfulness
is shaping generations.*

# CONTENTS

# INTRODUCTION

Fatherhood is one of the greatest honors a man can have—and one of the greatest challenges. It's not just about providing or protecting. It's about leading with purpose, loving with humility, and leaving behind a legacy that reflects God's truth.

In a world that often celebrates temporary success and shifting values, God calls fathers to something deeper: steadfast faith, courageous character, and spiritual leadership. He's not looking for perfection. He's looking for *willing men*—men who will stand in the gap, kneel in prayer, speak life into their families, and walk with integrity when no one is watching.

That's what this devotional is all about.

*Strength for the Journey* isn't a list of rules or religious checkboxes. It's a journey—30 days of scripture, reflection, prayer, and real-life challenges designed to help you live out your faith as a father. Each day is short enough to fit into your busy schedule, but deep enough to strengthen your spirit.

You may be a new dad learning the ropes, a grandfather passing down wisdom, or a man mentoring the next generation. No matter your stage in life, your influence matters more than you think.

This isn't just about being a good man. It's about being a Godly one.

So grab a cup of coffee. Open your Bible. Take five to ten minutes each day. Let God speak into your heart, shape your hands, and steady your soul.

Your children will remember your love.

Your family will follow your example.
Your legacy begins now.

Let's build it—together.

Karen

# LET'S LIVE IN CHRIST

# WEEK 1: FOUNDATION OF FAITH

Built on the Rock – Matthew 7:24

A Father's Armor – Ephesians 6:11

Strength in the Lord – Psalm 18:32

Walking in Integrity – Proverbs 20:7

Fear Not – Isaiah 41:10

A Quiet Strength – Ecclesiastes 9:17

Faithful in the Small – Luke 16:10

# DAY 1: BUILT ON THE ROCK

## Scripture

"Therefore whosoever heareth these sayings of mine, and doeth them, I will liken him unto a wise man, which built his house upon a rock."
— Matthew 7:24 (KJV)

## Reflection

Fatherhood is like building a house—every choice is a brick, every word a nail. But even the strongest house will collapse if it's not built on a solid foundation. Jesus reminds us that hearing His words is not enough—we must live by them.

As a father, your life is a blueprint for your family. When storms come—and they will—it's your faith that will hold the walls in place. Start each day with Christ as your cornerstone. When your children see you turn to God in both success and struggle, they learn what it means to build on the Rock.

## Prayer

Lord, help me be a wise builder.  Let Your Word guide my every decision and shape my character.  May my life be a testimony of Your strength and stability. Amen.

# *Challenge*

Spend five minutes today reading a Psalm aloud with your children. Let them hear God's Word from your voice.

# DAY 2: A FATHER'S ARMOR

## *Scripture*

"Put on the whole armour of God, that ye may be able to stand against the wiles of the devil."
— *Ephesians 6:11 (KJV)*

## *Reflection*

Every day you step into a battlefield—not with swords or shields, but with responsibilities, temptations, and unseen spiritual challenges. God didn't call you to fight empty-handed. He equipped you with truth, righteousness, peace, faith, salvation, and His Word. This is your armor.

As a father, you're not just protecting yourself—you're standing in the gap for your family. When you wake up each morning and put on God's armor through prayer and Scripture, you become a living defense against the darkness trying to creep into your home.

Suit up, Dad. Your example is how your children learn to stand strong.

## *Prayer*

Lord, I know I can't face this world on my own. Help me to put on Your armor daily.  Let me be a protector, a truth-bearer, and a warrior in faith for my family. Amen.

## Challenge

Pray Ephesians 6:10–18 aloud before starting your day. Invite your children to listen or join you if they can.

# DAY 3: STRENGTH IN THE LORD



## Scripture

"It is God that girdeth me with strength, and maketh my way perfect."
— *Psalm 18:32 (KJV)*

## Reflection

Strength doesn't always look like muscle. Sometimes it looks like a man holding back anger, choosing grace over pride, or staying faithful when quitting would be easier. True strength—lasting, steady, spiritual strength—comes from the Lord. David, a warrior and king, knew this. He didn't boast in his own ability. He gave credit to the One who empowered him.

As a father, lean on God. You weren't made to carry the weight of the world alone. Let Him gird you with strength that doesn't wear out at the end of a long day.

## Prayer

Father, I admit my strength runs out, but Yours never does. Fill me with Your power today. Help me lead with humility and rely on

You for every need. Amen.

## *Challenge:*

List three ways you've tried to handle life alone. Surrender each one to God in prayer today.

# DAY 4: WALKING IN INTEGRITY

*Scripture*

"The just man walketh in his integrity: his children are blessed after him."
—*Proverbs 20:7 (KJV)*

*Reflection*

Your children are watching—not just what you say, but what you *do.* Integrity isn't about perfection. It's about consistency between what you believe and how you behave. It's how you respond when no one is looking.

When you walk in integrity, you leave a trail of blessing behind you. Your honesty, humility, and faithfulness become the ground your children stand on. It might not seem like a big deal now, but someday they'll look back and say, "My dad kept his word. He did the right thing—even when it was hard." That's a legacy no money can buy.

*Prayer*

Lord, make me a man of integrity.  Let my life be an example of honesty, humility, and faith.  May my children be blessed because I walked in Your truth. Amen.

## Challenge

Think of one area where you can be more consistent (speech, promises, finances, etc.). Take one step today to walk in integrity there.

# DAY 5: FEAR NOT

### *Scripture*

"Fear thou not; for I am with thee: be not dismayed; for I am thy God..."
—*Isaiah 41:10 (KJV)*

### *Reflection*

Fear creeps in through quiet doubts: *Am I doing enough? What if I fail my family?* God doesn't ask you to be fearless—He asks you to trust Him. Isaiah 41:10 is God's personal reassurance that you are not alone.

When fear knocks, faith answers. Not because you're enough, but because God is. Your children need to see that strength comes not from avoiding fear, but facing it with courage that comes from trust in the Lord. Be bold—not because of who you are, but because of who He is.

### *Prayer*

God, when fear rises, remind me that You are with me.  Be my strength, my peace, and my confidence.  I trust in Your promises. Amen.

### *Challenge*

Write Isaiah 41:10 on a note and place it where you'll see it daily. Let it be your battle cry.

# DAY 6: A QUIET STRENGTH

## *Scripture*

"The words of wise men are heard in quiet more than the cry of him that ruleth among fools."
— *Ecclesiastes 9:17 (KJV)*

## *Reflection*

Real strength doesn't always roar. Sometimes it whispers wisdom when the world is shouting nonsense. As fathers, we're tempted to think we must be loud to be heard or harsh to lead. But the Bible honors the man whose quiet words carry weight because they come from truth, not pride.

Your children don't need a tyrant—they need a steady voice, a patient ear, a wise heart. Your calm in the chaos becomes their safe place. The world yells. God's wisdom speaks gently.

## *Prayer*

Lord, help me lead with quiet strength. Teach me to listen more than I speak, and to guide my family with patience, humility, and grace. Amen.

# Challenge

Today, intentionally speak one truth or encouragement quietly and calmly, even if the moment feels tense.

# DAY 7: FAITHFUL IN THE SMALL

### Scripture

"He that is faithful in that which is least is faithful also in much…"
—*Luke 16:10 (KJV)*

### Reflection

It's easy to dream of doing big things for God. But true character is revealed in how we handle the little things—changing diapers, showing up to baseball practice, or praying for your child's cold at bedtime.

Jesus said if you're faithful in the small things, you'll be trusted with more. Your quiet acts of faithfulness are not unseen. God honors them, and your children are shaped by them. The little things? They're the foundation of the big legacy.

### Prayer

God, remind me that every small act of love and faith matters. Help me be faithful in the everyday tasks of fatherhood.  Let me reflect Your love even in the unnoticed moments. Amen.

## *Challenge*

Do one "small" thing today with great love—wash the dishes, pack a lunch, or pray for your child. Then thank God for the privilege.

# WEEK 2: LEADING WITH LOVE

The Father's Heart – Luke 15:20

Speak Life – Proverbs 18:21

Loving Like Christ – Ephesians 5:25

Patience in the Storm – James 1:19

A Tender Warrior – 1 Corinthians 16:13-14

Forgiveness is Strength – Matthew 6:14

Be Present – Deuteronomy 6:6-7

# DAY 8: THE FATHER'S HEART



### Scripture

"But when he was yet a great way off, his father saw him, and had compassion…"
— Luke 15:20 (KJV)

### Reflection

The parable of the prodigal son isn't just about a wayward child—it's a glimpse into the heart of a father who loves without limits. As men, we're often tempted to lead with authority or discipline, but Jesus shows us the power of compassion.

The father in this story runs—yes, runs—to meet his son. No lecture, no punishment, just grace. Let your children see that while you stand firm in truth, your arms are always open in love.

### *Prayer*

Father God, thank You for loving me when I don't deserve it. Teach me to lead my family with the same grace and compassion. May my home always reflect Your mercy. Amen.

# *Challenge*

Tell your child one reason you're proud of them today—without correcting or adding advice.

# DAY 9: SPEAK LIFE



*Scripture*

"Death and life are in the power of the tongue: and they that love it shall eat the fruit thereof."
—*Proverbs 18:21 (KJV)*

*Reflection*

Your words matter more than you know. They can build up or tear down. Encourage or wound. Heal or harden. As a father, your voice becomes the inner voice of your children. The words you speak today echo in their hearts tomorrow.

The Bible reminds us that our tongue holds the power of life and death. That means a simple "I'm proud of you" can water confidence. A quiet "I'm sorry" can repair trust. Speaking life is a habit—and it starts by first hearing from the Giver of life. When your heart is full of God's Word, your mouth can't help but reflect it.

*Prayer*

Lord, teach me to speak with grace and truth. Let my words give life to those I love. Help me use my voice to reflect Yours—steady, kind, and full of wisdom. Amen.

## *Challenge*

Give each of your children (or someone close) a sincere, specific word of encouragement today. Watch what your words can do.

# DAY 10: LOVING LIKE CHRIST

## *Scripture*

"Husbands, love your wives, even as Christ also loved the church, and gave himself for it."
—*Ephesians 5:25 (KJV)*

## *Reflection*

Jesus didn't just say He loved the church—He proved it by giving His life for her. That's the kind of love we're called to offer our wives. Not just affection or good intentions, but sacrifice. It's love that serves, forgives, listens, and leads gently.

The way you love your wife teaches your children about commitment, respect, and grace. Loving like Christ doesn't mean being passive—it means being active in choosing to serve, to uplift, and to protect. In a world that distorts love, your example becomes their truth.

## *Prayer*

Jesus, thank You for loving me with such depth and mercy. Help me love my wife the way You love—sacrificially, patiently, and faithfully. Let our marriage honor You. Amen.

## Challenge

Do one sacrificial act of love for your wife today—unprompted, unannounced. Let it be your way of saying, "I choose you."

# DAY 11: PATIENCE IN THE STORM

## *Scripture*

"Wherefore, my beloved brethren, let every man be swift to hear, slow to speak, slow to wrath."
—*James 1:19 (KJV)*

## *Reflection*

It's easy to be patient when life is smooth. But when the storm hits—when the kids are loud, the bills stack up, or emotions run high—your patience becomes a powerful witness.

James calls us to be *slow to speak* and *slow to wrath.* That's not weakness—it's godly strength under control. Your calm in chaos teaches your family how to respond when life doesn't go as planned. And often, the way you handle pressure leaves a deeper impact than anything you say.

## *Prayer*

Father, give me patience that reflects Your peace. Help me listen with care and speak with gentleness, even when I feel overwhelmed.

Fill my home with calm because of You. Amen.

## *Challenge*

In a stressful moment today, pause. Take a breath. Then respond slowly, with kindness—modeling what it means to be "slow to wrath."

# DAY 12: A TENDER WARRIOR

## Scripture

"Watch ye, stand fast in the faith, quit you like men, be strong. Let all your things be done with charity."
— *1 Corinthians 16:13–14 (KJV)*

## Reflection

Men are called to be both strong and tender. Warriors and protectors—but also servants and lovers. Paul reminds us to "be strong," but also to do everything "with charity"—with love. That's a powerful balance.

Your family doesn't just need a man who fights their battles—they need a man who fights for their hearts. You don't have to choose between strength and softness. Real masculinity is being tough enough to defend and humble enough to love well.

## Prayer

God, help me live as both a warrior and a servant. Give me the courage to stand firm and the humility to lead with love. Let my strength reflect Yours. Amen.

Do one bold, protective thing today (pray over your family, set a boundary), and one tender act (hug, listen, express love).

# DAY 13: FORGIVENESS IS STRENGTH



"For if ye forgive men their trespasses, your heavenly Father will also forgive you."
— *Matthew 6:14 (KJV)*

## Reflection

Forgiveness feels hard—but it's a sign of spiritual strength, not weakness. Jesus makes it clear: forgiving others is connected to the grace we receive. Holding onto bitterness is a heavy burden, but forgiveness frees both your heart and your home.

As a father, modeling forgiveness—whether to your spouse, your children, or yourself—shows your family what real grace looks like. Don't let your pride speak louder than your love. Remember how much you've been forgiven—and pass it on.

## Prayer

Father, help me let go of bitterness. Teach me to forgive quickly and love deeply. Let my heart be free so I can lead my family with grace. Amen.

## Challenge

If someone has wronged you—even in a small way—choose to forgive them today. Tell them if needed. If it's your child, forgive them openly and gently

# DAY 14: BE PRESENT



*Scripture*

"And these words, which I command thee this day, shall be in thine heart: And thou shalt teach them diligently unto thy children…"
— *Deuteronomy 6:6–7 (KJV)*

*Reflection*

God never designed fathers to be distant providers. He called them to be spiritual teachers, present in their children's daily lives. Teaching diligently means *showing up*—in the morning chaos, the bedtime routine, the car rides, and the messy moments.

You don't need to have all the answers. You just need to be available. Your consistent presence creates safety. And when God's Word is in your heart, it naturally overflows in your actions, your words, and the rhythm of your home.

*Prayer*

Lord, don't let me miss the moments that matter. Help me slow down, listen well, and be present with my family. Let my life reflect Your love in our home. Amen.

# *Challenge*

Put down your phone or step away from a task today and give your child your full attention—no distractions—for at least 15 minutes.

DAD

# WEEK 3: COURAGE AND CHARACTER

Be Strong and of Good Courage – Joshua 1:9

What Real Success Looks Like – Mark 8:36

Work as Unto the Lord – Colossians 3:23

Teach by Example – Titus 2:7

Guard Your Heart – Proverbs 4:23

When You Fall – Proverbs 24:16

True Manhood – Micah 6:8

# DAY 15: BE STRONG AND OF GOOD COURAGE

*Scripture*

"Have not I commanded thee? Be strong and of a good courage..."
—Joshua 1:9 (KJV)

*Reflection*

God didn't just encourage Joshua—He *commanded* him to be strong and courageous. Not because Joshua was fearless, but because God was with him. Courage isn't the absence of fear; it's choosing to act in faith despite fear. As fathers, we face challenges that test our patience, finances, marriages, and dreams. But God's promise to Joshua is ours too. Stand firm. Lead boldly. Your courage becomes your children's security.

*Prayer*

God, give me the strength to face what lies ahead. Let my children see not just a strong man, but a faithful one. Be with me in every step. Amen.

## Challenge

Write down one fear you're facing. Pray over it, and speak Joshua 1:9 aloud today.

# DAY 16: WHAT REAL SUCCESS LOOKS LIKE



"For what shall it profit a man, if he shall gain the whole world, and lose his own soul?"
— *Mark 8:36 (KJV)*

## *Reflection*

The world has a definition for success: more money, more power, more recognition. But Jesus offers a sobering reminder—success without your soul is no success at all.

As a father, it's easy to chase after promotions or possessions, thinking you're providing a better life. But the best life you can give your children is one anchored in eternal values: love, integrity, and faith.

Success isn't just about what you achieve. It's about *who you become.* And when you lead with your soul, your family learns what real treasure looks like.

## *Prayer*

Lord, help me keep my eyes on eternal things. Let me seek Your approval above all else. Teach me to lead my family not just to success—but to You. Amen.

## Challenge

Ask yourself: What does success look like in God's eyes? Write down 3 eternal goals you want to pursue as a man of faith.

# DAY 17: WORK AS UNTO THE LORD



*Scripture*

"And whatsoever ye do, do it heartily, as to the Lord, and not unto men;"
— *Colossians 3:23 (KJV)*

*Reflection*

Whether you wear a suit, swing a hammer, or manage your home—your work matters to God. Every task is sacred when it's done for Him.

God doesn't measure your worth by your title. He looks at your heart. When you work with excellence and humility, you set an example for your children: that every role is a calling, and every job can bring glory to God.

So take pride in your work—not for applause, but because it's an offering.

*Prayer*

Father, help me work with diligence and joy. Whether I'm seen or unnoticed, let me serve with excellence and bring honor to You. Amen.

## Challenge

Pick one task today—big or small—and do it wholeheartedly. Before you begin, whisper: "This is for You, Lord."

# DAY 18: TEACH BY EXAMPLE

*Scripture*

"In all things shewing thyself a pattern of good works: in doctrine shewing uncorruptness, gravity, sincerity,"
— *Titus 2:7 (KJV)*

*Reflection*

Children may not always listen to what you say—but they never miss what you *do.* Your example is your loudest sermon.

Whether you're praying at the dinner table, showing patience when you're frustrated, or offering forgiveness, your kids are learning: *This is how a godly man lives.* You don't have to be perfect, just consistent.

Live in a way that says: "Follow me as I follow Christ." That kind of example speaks louder than a thousand lectures.

*Prayer*

Lord, let my life be a living example of Your truth. Help me model integrity, humility, and grace—so that my children see You in me.

Amen.

## Challenge

42

Choose one godly trait you want to model better (honesty, patience, etc.). Make one decision today that reflects that trait in action.

# DAY 19: GUARD YOUR HEART

*Scripture*

"Keep thy heart with all diligence; for out of it are the issues of life."
— Proverbs 4:23 (KJV)

*Reflection*

Your heart is the wellspring of your thoughts, your words, your actions. If you let bitterness, lust, or pride creep in, it won't stay hidden—it will overflow.

As a father, guarding your heart is one of the most powerful ways to protect your family. Your children don't just learn from what you say; they absorb who you are. Protect your heart through prayer, accountability, and time in God's Word. A clean heart sets the tone for a peaceful home.

*Prayer*

Lord, create in me a clean heart and renew a right spirit within me. Let me be a man of purity, peace, and purpose. Amen.

# *Challenge*

Choose one verse to memorize with your child this week. Let it shape your hearts together.

# DAY 20: WHEN YOU FALL

## *Scripture*

"For a just man falleth seven times, and riseth up again: but the wicked shall fall into mischief."
—*Proverbs 24:16 (KJV)*

## *Reflection*

Falling doesn't make you a failure. Staying down does. The Bible doesn't say the righteous never fall—it says they *get back up.*

As a father, your family isn't watching for perfection. They're watching how you respond when you mess up. Do you own your mistakes? Do you ask for forgiveness? Do you keep going?

Strength isn't found in never falling. It's found in the courage to rise again, lean on God, and walk forward with humility and hope.

## *Prayer*

God, I've stumbled. But I thank You for grace that lifts me up. Give me strength to rise, wisdom to grow, and humility to keep moving forward. Amen.

# Challenge

Share a moment with your child (or loved one) when you failed—
but got back up. Let them see that falling is human, and rising is
faith.

# DAY 21: TRUE MANHOOD

*Scripture*

"He hath shewed thee, O man, what is good; and what doth the Lord require of thee, but to do justly, and to love mercy, and to walk humbly with thy God?"
— *Micah 6:8 (KJV)*

*Reflection*

The world offers a warped image of manhood—domination, wealth, pride. But God gives a different blueprint: justice, mercy, and humility.

True manhood isn't loud or showy. It's lived out in quiet strength, selfless love, and a heart that walks close to God. A man who defends the weak, shows compassion, and admits when he's wrong—that's the kind of man who leaves a godly legacy.

And your children? They're watching, learning what it means to be strong *and* good.

*Prayer*

Father, shape me into the man You've called me to be. Let me live justly, love mercy, and walk humbly with You every day. Amen.

## Challenge

Write Micah 6:8 on a card or note. Put it where you'll see it—on your desk, dashboard, or mirror—and make it your daily aim.

# WEEK 4: LEGACY AND LEADERSHIP

Generational Impact – Psalm 112:1-2

A Father's Words – Proverbs 1:8-9

Faith in Action – James 2:17

Passing the Torch – 2 Timothy 2:2

Trusting God's Timing – Ecclesiastes 3:1

Praying for Your Children – Job 1:5

Keep Your Eyes on the Prize – Hebrews 12:1-2

Stand Firm – 1 Corinthians 15:58

Finish Well – 2 Timothy 4:7

# DAY 22: GENERATIONAL IMPACT

## Scripture

"Praise ye the Lord. Blessed is the man that feareth the Lord, that delighteth greatly in his commandments. His seed shall be mighty upon earth: the generation of the upright shall be blessed."
—*Psalm 112:1–2 (KJV)*

## Reflection

Your faith doesn't end with you—it echoes into future generations. The way you live, love, pray, and lead today can influence your children, your grandchildren, and even those yet unborn.

God promises that the man who fears the Lord and loves His commandments leaves behind a blessed legacy. Your quiet obedience today becomes your children's spiritual inheritance tomorrow.

You may never be famous in the world's eyes, but in your family tree, your faith may be the turning point that shapes generations.

Lord, help me live in a way that blesses my children and the generations to come. May my life be a link in a godly chain that reaches far beyond what I can see. Amen.

## *Challenge*

Write a note to your child or grandchild, expressing your hopes for their walk with God. Tuck it into a Bible or keepsake box.

# DAY 23: A FATHER'S WORDS

## Scripture

"My son, hear the instruction of thy father, and forsake not the law of thy mother: For they shall be an ornament of grace unto thy head, and chains about thy neck."
— *Proverbs 1:8–9 (KJV)*

## Reflection

Your words matter—especially to your children. They will carry your voice in their minds long after they leave your home.

Solomon urges sons to treasure a father's instruction like a crown of wisdom. That means your words can either uplift or undermine, bless or burden.

Speak truth. Speak blessing. Speak life. Your tone teaches love or fear. Your words shape self-worth and confidence. The way you instruct, correct, and affirm will echo for years.

*Prayer*

Father, help me use my words wisely. Let them be full of grace, wisdom, and love. May my instruction lead my children closer to You. Amen.

## Challenge

Today, speak a blessing over your child aloud—something personal, specific, and rooted in God's Word.

# DAY 24: FAITH IN ACTION

## Scripture

"Even so faith, if it hath not works, is dead, being alone."
—*James 2:17 (KJV)*

## Reflection

You can say you believe in God—but what do your actions say? James reminds us that real faith moves. It serves. It sacrifices. It obeys.

As a father, your actions show your children what it means to follow Jesus. They'll see how you spend your time, treat others, and respond to trials. That's where your faith is tested—and proven.

Faith isn't just what you believe. It's what you *do* because you believe. So let your life speak louder than your words.

## Prayer

Lord, let my faith be alive and active. Show me where I need to move, give, or serve. May my actions reflect my trust in You. Amen.

## Challenge

Do one act of service today that puts your faith into action—something your children can see and learn from.

# DAY 25: PASSING THE TORCH

## Scripture

"And the things that thou hast heard of me among many witnesses, the same commit thou to faithful men, who shall be able to teach others also."
—*2 Timothy 2:2 (KJV)*

## Reflection

Paul didn't just teach Timothy—he trained him to teach others. That's how legacies grow: when what we've learned is passed down with purpose.

You're not just raising children. You're raising future leaders, husbands, wives, and disciples. Don't just correct behavior—shape hearts. Don't just provide—invest in their souls.

When you pass on your faith, your values, and your love for God, you're lighting a torch that can burn long after you're gone.

## Prayer

God, help me be intentional in passing my faith to the next generation. Let me be a teacher, mentor, and father who multiplies truth. Amen.

## Challenge

Have a spiritual conversation with your child today. Share a story of how God has worked in your life.

# DAY 26: TRUSTING GOD'S TIMING

*Scripture*

"To every thing there is a season, and a time to every purpose under the heaven:"
—*Ecclesiastes 3:1 (KJV)*

*Reflection*

We often want answers now. Results now. Change now. But God works in seasons—and His timing is perfect.

As a father, you may be waiting on something big: your child's salvation, a healing, a breakthrough. Don't give up. Trust that God sees the whole story. Your job is not to rush Him—it's to remain faithful while you wait.

When you model patience and peace in God's timing, your family learns that life isn't about instant gratification, but faithful trust.

*Prayer*

Lord, remind me that Your timing is always good. Teach me to wait with hope, to trust with peace, and to live faithfully in every season. Amen.

## Challenge

Share a story with your family about a time you had to wait on God—and how He came through.

# DAY 27: PRAYING FOR YOUR CHILDREN

## *Scripture*

"And it was so, when the days of their feasting were gone about, that Job sent and sanctified them… Thus did Job continually."
—*Job 1:5 (KJV)*

## *Reflection*

Before trouble came, Job was already praying. Not out of fear—but out of faith. He interceded daily for his children, offering sacrifices and lifting them to God.

As a father, one of your greatest roles is that of a prayer warrior. You may not always be able to protect your children from the world—but you can cover them in prayer.

Make prayer a daily rhythm. It may not be seen, but it will be felt. And heaven will remember every word.

## *Prayer*

Father, thank You for my children. I lift them up to You today—bless them, protect them, and draw them near to You. Make me faithful in prayer. Amen.

## Challenge

Write down your children's names and one prayer for each. Start a habit of praying over them by name each day.

# DAY 28: KEEP YOUR EYES ON THE PRIZE

*Scripture*

"Let us run with patience the race that is set before us, Looking unto Jesus the author and finisher of our faith..."
—*Hebrews 12:1–2 (KJV)*

*Reflection*

Life is a race—not a sprint, but a marathon. And the only way to run it well is to keep your eyes on Jesus.

Distractions will come. Setbacks will happen. But when your focus stays on Christ, you'll find the strength to keep going.

Your children are watching you run. They're learning how to persevere, how to worship through weariness, and how to keep the faith. Run for the One who already won the victory—and invite your family to run with you.

*Prayer*

Jesus, help me stay focused. In every joy and every hardship, remind me that You are the goal. Help me run with endurance and leave a path of faith behind me. Amen.

## Challenge

What's distracting you from God right now? Remove one distraction today and fix your eyes on Christ.

# DAY 29: STAND FIRM

## *Scripture*

"Therefore, my beloved brethren, be ye stedfast, unmoveable, always abounding in the work of the Lord..."
— *1 Corinthians 15:58 (KJV)*

## *Reflection*

This world is full of shifting sands—changing values, temporary pleasures, and constant pressure to conform. But God calls you to stand firm.

Steadfast. Unmovable. That's the kind of father your family needs. One who doesn't waver with the winds of culture or emotion, but who stays rooted in the truth of God's Word.

Being steadfast isn't easy—but it is powerful. When your children see you standing firm in faith, they'll know where to turn when the storms come.

## *Prayer*

Lord, anchor me in Your truth. Help me be steadfast when it's hard, unshaken when it's unpopular, and always faithful to Your calling. Amen.

## Challenge

Identify one area where you've felt tempted to compromise. Choose today to stand firm—by God's grace.

# DAY 30: FINISH WELL

## Scripture

"I have fought a good fight, I have finished my course, I have kept the faith."
— 2 Timothy 4:7 (KJV)

## Reflection

Every father leaves a legacy—but the kind you leave is up to you. Paul's final words are a declaration of victory—not of wealth or comfort, but of faithfulness. You don't have to be a perfect dad. You just have to finish well. Be the man who keeps showing up. The one who repents quickly, forgives freely, and loves sacrificially. Run the race with endurance. Someday your children will look back and say, "My dad kept the faith."

## Prayer

Father, help me finish well. When I grow weary, strengthen me. When I stumble, lift me. May my legacy be one of faith that points to You. Amen.

Write a letter to your child (or record a video) about the faith you want to pass down. Save it for them as a keepsake.

# REFLECTION

The following reflection questions are designed to be used at the end of each week, allowing fathers to contemplate the week's lessons and apply them practically. Incorporating these into your devotional book will provide readers with a structured path to deeper spiritual growth and intentional fatherhood.

# WEEK 1: THE CALL TO FATHERHOOD

How do I perceive God's calling in my role as a father?

In what ways have I embraced or resisted this calling?

What fears or insecurities do I need to surrender to God regarding fatherhood?

How can I model God's love and patience to my children?

What steps can I take this week to be more intentional in my parenting?

# WEEK 2: STRENGTH AND INTEGRITY

Where have I demonstrated strength in my fatherhood journey?

Are there areas where I need to cultivate greater integrity?

How does my character influence my children's spiritual growth?

What habits can I develop to align more closely with God's standards?

Who can I seek accountability from to maintain integrity in my actions?

# WEEK 3: LOVE AND LEADERSHIP

How do I balance love and discipline in my parenting approach?

In what ways can I lead my family spiritually this week?

What does servant leadership look like in my household?

How can I encourage my children to develop their own relationship with God?

What legacy of faith am I building for future generations?

# WEEK 4: LEGACY AND LEADERSHIP

What values do I want to instill in my children that reflect God's truth?

How can I demonstrate forgiveness and grace in my family relationships?

In what ways am I preparing my children to face spiritual challenges?

How do I model trust in God's timing and plans?

What traditions or practices can I establish to strengthen our family's faith journey?

# JOURNALING PROMPTS

*for Christian Fathers*

These prompts are designed to encourage introspection and growth in your role as a father. By regularly engaging with these questions, you can deepen your relationship with God and your family, fostering a legacy rooted in faith and love.

1. **Reflecting on God's Calling:**
   - *How has God uniquely called me to lead my family? In what ways am I embracing or resisting this calling?*

2. **Demonstrating Christ-like Love:**
   - *In what ways do I show unconditional love to my children? How can I better mirror Christ's love in my parenting?*

3. **Balancing Strength and Gentleness:**
   - *How do I balance being a strong protector with showing gentleness and compassion? Are there areas where I lean too heavily on one over the other?*

4. **Modeling Integrity:**
   - *Am I living a life of integrity that my children can emulate? What specific actions*

*can I take to strengthen this aspect of my character?*

### 5. Navigating Challenges with Faith:

- *Describe a recent challenge in fatherhood. How did my faith influence my response, and what did I learn from the experience?*

### 6. Cultivating Patience:

- *In moments of frustration, how do I practice patience? What scriptures or prayers help me remain calm and understanding?*

### 7. Encouraging Spiritual Growth:

- *What steps am I taking to nurture the spiritual growth of my children? How can I create more opportunities for faith-based conversations?*

### 8. Leaving a Legacy:

- *What kind of spiritual legacy do I want to leave for my family? What daily actions contribute to building this legacy?*

### 9. Seeking God's Guidance:

- *In what areas of fatherhood do I need God's guidance the most? How am I actively seeking His wisdom in these areas?*

### 10. Expressing Gratitude:

- *What blessings have I experienced in my role as a father? How can I express gratitude to God and my family for these gifts?*

# ACTION PLANS

By implementing these action plans, fathers can actively live out the principles discussed in each week's devotionals, leading their families with intentionality and faith.

# WEEK 1: THE CALL TO FATHERHOOD

**Theme:** Embracing the sacred responsibility and privilege of being a father.

1. **Initiate a Family Devotion Night**
   - Set aside one evening this week for a short family devotion. Choose a simple Bible passage, read it together, and discuss its relevance to your family life.

2. **Write a Personal Mission Statement**
   - Reflect on your role as a father and write a brief mission statement outlining your commitment to leading your family in faith and love.

3. **Schedule One-on-One Time with Each Child**
   - Plan individual time with each of your children this week to engage in activities they enjoy, fostering

# WEEK 2: STRENGTH AND INTEGRITY

**Theme:** Building character and leading by example.

1. **Demonstrate Integrity in Daily Decisions**
   - Identify an area where you can model integrity—such as honesty in communication or fairness in discipline—and consciously practice it throughout the week.

2. **Share a Personal Testimony**
   - Share a story with your children about a time when you had to make a tough decision to do the right thing, emphasizing the importance of integrity.

3. **Set a Personal Growth Goal**

   - Choose an area for personal development (e.g., patience, humility) and create a plan to work on it, demonstrating continuous growth to your family.

# WEEK 3: LOVE AND LEADERSHIP

**Theme:** Leading the family with love, humility, and purpose.

1. **Plan a One-on-One Activity**
   - Spend quality time individually with each child, engaging in an activity they enjoy, to strengthen your bond and demonstrate your love.

2. **Lead a Family Prayer Time**
   - Gather your family for a dedicated prayer session, encouraging each member to share prayer requests and pray for one another.

3. **Write a Letter of Affirmation**
   - Write a heartfelt letter to each of your children, expressing your love, pride, and hopes for their future.

# WEEK 4: LEGACY AND LEADERSHIP

**Theme:** Leaving a lasting spiritual legacy.

1. **Create a Family Vision Board**
   - Collaborate with your family to create a visual representation of your collective goals, values, and dreams, reinforcing a shared vision for your family's future.

2. **Establish a Weekly Family Meeting**
   - Set a regular time each week to discuss family matters, celebrate achievements, and address concerns, fostering open communication and unity.

3. **Document Family Traditions**
   - Write down your family's traditions and the stories behind them, preserving them for future generations.

# PRAYERS

These prayers are designed to resonate with fathers at various stages of their journey, offering comfort, guidance, and a deeper connection to their faith. Incorporating them into your devotional book can provide readers with practical tools to navigate the complexities of fatherhood with spiritual insight.

# PRAYER FOR WISDOM

**Lord God,**

You are the source of all wisdom. As I navigate the responsibilities of being a father, I seek Your guidance. Grant me discernment in decisions, clarity in confusion, and insight in challenges. Help me to lead my family not by my own understanding, but by the wisdom that comes from You. May my choices reflect Your will, and may I be a beacon of Your truth to my children.

In Your holy name,
Amen.

# PRAYER FOR PROTECTION OVER MY CHILDREN

**Father of All,**

I entrust my children into Your loving care. Shield them from harm, both seen and unseen. Protect their hearts from discouragement, their minds from deceit, and their bodies from danger. Surround them with Your angels, and let Your presence be their constant companion. Guide their steps, Lord, and keep them safe in Your embrace.

Through Christ our Lord,
Amen.

# PRAYER FOR STRENGTH IN TRIALS

**Mighty God,**

In times of trial and uncertainty, I turn to You for strength. When challenges arise in my role as a father, fortify me with courage and resilience. Help me to stand firm in faith, to persevere with hope, and to lead my family with unwavering trust in Your promises. Remind me that in my weakness, Your strength is made perfect.

In Jesus' name,
Amen.

# PRAYER FOR LEGACY AND IMPACT

**Eternal Father,**

I desire to leave a legacy that honors You. May my life be a testament to Your grace and truth. Help me to instill values of faith, love, and integrity in my children. Let my actions inspire them to seek You wholeheartedly. Use me as an instrument to shape not just their lives, but the generations to come. May my legacy be one that reflects Your glory.

In Your precious name,
Amen.

# RECOMMENDED READING LIST FOR CHRISTIAN FATHERS

These books offer a wealth of knowledge and practical advice for fathers striving to lead their families in faith and integrity. Incorporating them into your reading can further enrich your journey through *Strength for the Journey.*

1. **The Intentional Father** by Jon Tyson
   A practical guide offering activities and rites of passage to help fathers raise sons of courage and character.

2. **Faith Training: Raising Kids Who Love the Lord** by Dr. Joe White
   Provides daily devotional thoughts and discussion questions to effectively disciple children.

3. **A Practical Guide for Praying Parents** by Dr. Erwin Lutzer
   Offers scriptural prayers to bless children and bring parents closer to God.

4. **Raising a Modern-Day Knight** by Robert Lewis
   Outlines a vision for raising sons into authentic manhood through biblical principles.

5. **Shepherding a Child's Heart** by Tedd Tripp
   Focuses on shaping a child's heart rather than just correcting behavior.

6. **The Power of a Praying Parent** by Stormie Omartian
   Guides parents in praying effectively for their children's lives.

7. **Bringing Up Boys** by Dr. James Dobson
   Addresses the challenges of raising boys in today's culture with biblical wisdom.

8. **Disciplines of a Godly Man** by R. Kent Hughes
   Encourages men to pursue spiritual disciplines to grow in godliness.

9. **The Resolution for Men** by Stephen and Alex Kendrick
   Challenges men to embrace their roles as leaders in their homes and communities.

10. **Fathered by God** by John Eldredge
    Explores the stages of a man's life and how God fathers men through each stage.

11. **Parenting: 14 Gospel Principles That Can Radically Change Your Family** by Paul David Tripp
Provides a gospel-centered approach to parenting.

12. **Dare to Discipline** by Dr. James Dobson
Offers practical advice on disciplining children with love and consistency.

13. **The 5 Love Languages of Children** by Gary Chapman and Ross Campbell
Helps parents understand and speak their child's love language.

14. **King Me: What Every Son Wants and Needs from His Father** by Steve Farrar
Encourages fathers to be the role models their sons need.

15. **Lead: 12 Gospel Principles for Leadership in the Church** by Paul David Tripp
Applies gospel principles to leadership roles, including within the family.

16. **The Dad Difference** by Bryan Loritts
Highlights the unique role fathers play in shaping their children's lives.

17. **Man Enough: How Jesus Redefines Manhood** by Nate Pyle
Challenges cultural norms and presents a Christ-centered view of manhood.

18. **The Blessing** by John Trent and Gary Smalley
Discusses the importance of affirming children through the biblical concept of blessing.

19. **Strong Fathers, Strong Daughters** by Dr. Meg Meeker
Emphasizes the critical role fathers play in their daughters' lives.

20. **Point Man: How a Man Can Lead His Family** by Steve Farrar

Encourages men to take spiritual leadership in their homes.

# CLOSING PRAYER

**Heavenly Father,**

As I conclude this 30-day journey, I pause to thank You for walking beside me. Through each reflection, Scripture, and prayer, You have spoken to my heart, challenged my spirit, and reminded me of the sacred calling of fatherhood.

Lord, I acknowledge that I cannot fulfill this role in my own strength. I need Your guidance to lead with wisdom, Your love to nurture with compassion, and Your grace to persevere through challenges. Mold me into the father You desire me to be—a man of integrity, faith, and unwavering commitment.

Help me to be present in my children's lives, to listen intently, and to speak words that build up and inspire. May my actions reflect Your love, and may my legacy be one that points my family toward You.

Thank You for entrusting me with the gift of fatherhood. I commit to walking this path with humility, courage, and reliance on Your strength.

In Jesus' name, I pray. Amen.

# ACKNOWLEDGEMENT

I could not write books without you, the reader.

I enjoy each and all comments.  My email address is:

authorkarenshockley@gmail.com.

You can also visit my web page at www.karenswords.com

or follow me on my FaceBook page for
upcoming information and deals.

https://www.facebook.com/angelstoriesbook

# GRACE FOR EVERY SEASON

Discover the perfect companion for celebrating life's most meaningful moments with Grace for Every Season, a heartfelt series dedicated to bringing faith and inspiration to special occasions. Whether it's the joy of a wedding day, the solemnity of a memorial service, or the warmth of a holiday gathering, this series combines thoughtfully selected Bible verses, reflective insights, and soul-stirring prayers to honor every event.

Each volume is tailored to specific themes, including milestones, holidays, and seasons of life, ensuring a message of hope and encouragement is always close at hand. From uplifting passages to guide new beginnings, to gentle reminders of God's love during challenging times, Grace for Every Season is a celebration of His presence in all moments, big and small.

Perfect for personal devotion, group prayer, or as a gift to share with others, this series offers timeless wisdom and spiritual guidance to inspire hearts and unite communities. With its thoughtful blend of scripture, reflection, and prayer, Grace for Every Season invites readers to experience God's grace anew, whenever and wherever life unfolds.

## God's Design For Her (Grace For Every Season Book 1)

Find Strength, Grace, and Encouragement—One Week at a Time

Life is busy, but your faith journey matters. God's Design For Her: 52 Bible Verses for Women is a year-long devotional designed to uplift and inspire you. Each week, you'll find a carefully chosen Bible verse, a thoughtful reflection, and a heartfelt prayer —all created to help you grow in faith, embrace your God-given purpose, and walk confidently in His love.

Whether you're seeking peace, wisdom, or encouragement, this book will remind you that you are cherished, strong, and never alone. Take a few moments each week to draw closer to God and discover the beauty of His promises for you.

Start your journey today—because His grace is with you, every step of the way.

## Not Just January: 52 Weekly Devotions To Begin Today (Grace For Every Season Book 2)

Begin your year—any time of the year—with the timeless truths of God's Word.

Experience a full year of encouragement, one week at a time, through 52 handpicked verses from the King James Bible—each one beautifully paired with reflections that invite you into deeper faith, renewed hope, abiding love, and joyful celebration.

Whether you're beginning in January or starting fresh in June, this devotional is designed with flexibility in mind. Each weekly entry features:

A powerful Bible verse from the beloved King James Version

An uplifting reflection to help you connect the verse to your daily life

A spiritual focus—Faith, Hope, Love, or Celebration—to guide your week

Encouragement and application to draw you closer to God

Perfect for morning devotionals, weekly quiet time, or as a

thoughtful gift for a friend, this book will become a cherished companion on your walk with the Lord.

No matter the day or season, there's always time to grow your faith. Let this devotional remind you: You can start today.

## Daily Scriptures, Devotions And Prayers To Uplift A Mother's Heart : A Month Of Hope And Strength (Grace For Every Season Book 3)

You are seen. You are strong. You are deeply loved.

In the everyday moments of motherhood—where laundry piles up, sleep is scarce, and love is poured out in countless quiet ways—it's easy to feel overwhelmed or overlooked. But God sees you, and He is with you in every moment.

This 30-day devotional is a heartfelt companion for mothers in all seasons of life. Each day features a powerful Scripture from the King James Version, a thoughtful devotional reflection, a heartfelt prayer, and a simple, meaningful activity designed to help you grow in faith, find peace in the chaos, and rediscover the beauty of your calling.

Whether you're a new mom, a seasoned parent, or somewhere in between, this devotional will encourage your soul, strengthen your spirit, and remind you of this truth: you are never alone—and your work as a mother has eternal significance.

## Love Fully: 30 Days Of Scripture, Prayer & Purpose (Grace For Every Season Book 4)

Experience the power of love—God's way.

In a fast-paced world full of distraction and pressure, Love Fully: 30 Days of Scripture, Prayer & Purpose invites you to slow down and reconnect with what truly matters. This beautiful devotional offers a month-long journey through 30 powerful scriptures from the King James Bible, each paired with a devotional thought, a heartfelt prayer, and a simple love-centered activity.

Whether you're looking to deepen your faith, strengthen your relationships, or simply live more intentionally, this book is for you. You'll explore God's love for you, learn how to love others with grace and patience, and discover how small acts of kindness can create lasting change.

Written with warmth, encouragement, and spiritual depth, Love Fully: 30 Days of Scripture, Prayer & Purpose is perfect for women of all ages, Bible study groups, or anyone seeking a daily dose of love, faith, and truth.
Come rest in His love. Reflect His heart. Live it out—one day at a time.